To:

_____

From:

_____

May this book help you find
Rays of hope and comfort
For your grieving heart

RAYS OF HOPE IN TIMES OF LOSS

courage and comfort for grieving hearts

Susan Zimmerman, LMFT, ChFC

Expert Publishing, Inc.
Andover, Minnesota

Photography by Susan G. Zimmerman and Kathryn Galloway

ISBN 10: 1-931945-35-7
ISBN 13: 978-1-931945-35-6

Library of Congress Catalog Number: 2005925595

Printed in South Korea

First Printing: April 2005

08 07 06 05   6 5 4 3 2 1

Expert Publishing, Inc.
14314 Thrush Street NW
Andover, MN 55304-3330
1-877-755-4966
www.expertpublishinginc.com

This book
is
dedicated
to
the memory
of

JESSICA JUNE

We wonder if there's a ray of hope,
While fearing we can't possibly cope.

Lost in mourning, we're unsure what to seek,
But if we keep searching, sometimes braving a peek,

Two miracles will appear in a heartening blend,
One we'll find in nature, the other in a Friend.

As you read the poems in this book, my wish is that you find courage and comfort for your grieving heart in their honesty and message of hope. Life transitions or losing a loved one can be a painful and difficult experience and we may need to be open to more creative outlets than our usual coping methods have offered in the past to help us through. Create and keep many channels of communication open and miracles will hearten you in your journey.

"What we have once enjoyed we can never lose...
all that we love deeply becomes a part of us."
—Helen Keller

The poems in *Rays of Hope in Times of Loss* reflect different aspects of the emotional excursion through grief. They help us see the glimmers of hope in the transformational potential inherent in healthy mourning of a loss. Some poems may give you ideas about additional ways you can move through your grief with ceremonies or symbols that honor treasured memories. Others may provide validation of feelings you have had but did not feel comfortable sharing.

I created *Rays of Hope in Times of Loss* also for the caring people who wish to help console a grieving person. It is a gift book that can be given to help you express your sympathy, support, and love.

In the book *Poetic Medicine*, John Fox writes:

> *Poems speak to us when nothing else will... Reading poetry during difficult times may be a great comfort. People have told me reading poetry was the only thing they could do to make it through the brambles of their grief. A woman told me that only poetry was pure enough to soothe her.*

A poem can be a comforting companion in your journey through grief. Like a painting or photograph, it can touch your heart in a way that ordinary words cannot. It can help you reach that place that needed to be found deep inside you. It can help you cry, but it can also help you laugh again. Sometimes it can make you sigh, relax, and breathe healthier, deep breaths. It can bring a needed insight that encourages your movement through the loss of a loved one or other difficult life transitions. A single word, rhyme, or rhythm can create a soothing sensation or be a pleasing surprise. All that is required is attention and an open heart and desire to honor your grief, rather than deny it.

When to Seek Help

Although this book's purpose is to help people find courage and comfort in their times of grieving, it is not a substitute for therapy. Please seek assistance from a mental health professional if you experience a persistent, depressed sense of total despair or a feeling that you don't value your own life. Substituting alcohol, drugs, overeating, or other unhealthy behaviors can result if you are unable to accept the death or loss. Your life holds value and the world needs your unique gifts. Professional guidance can help you move through your grief and rebuild your life so you can again find joy and live in a productive way.

Loss is something we all experience in life, yet we have received precious little education about how to grieve significant losses in healthy, helpful ways. American culture, in fact, has a tendency to try and rush past it and attempt to avoid the natural suffering that loss and change entails. Grief, in its simplest definition, is deep sadness or emotional distress.

In current American culture our own suffering may be intensified due to myths about youth, success, and materialism. We may find enlightenment in our movement through grief by challenging the myth that we can ignore, control or opt out of grief.

Especially when a loss is sudden or unexpected, our resistance to suffering leaves us poorly equipped to cope. We discover that, to some extent, we have bought into the American belief that painful emotions or circumstances are optional. We mistakenly believe we should be able to get busy and escape our pain and that the faster we ignore it, the better off we'll be. But when this is what is practiced, all too often our unacknowledged grief may manifest in other ways, including health problems or behaviors that hurt those we love the most. Perhaps *Rays of Hope* can help prevent such unnecessary disharmony and difficulty. It cannot eliminate the pain of grief, but can help us move through it.

I found my way to a quiet place,
intent to not speak a word.
And then came the soothing voice of Grace,
who inspired me to be heard.

2

People vary in their need for expression in times of grief. Some people are more naturally verbal than others. Most need some outlet to express their sorrow at one time or another, even if it is brief. There may be times when you end up sharing an aspect of your grief that you hadn't intended, and it becomes a gift of simple validation, as we see in the poem "A Touch of Grace." Learning to trust in our own sharing can be a valuable discovery, one for which the risk was worth taking.

Simple in its message, "Faithful Courage" reminds us that faith is an important part of finding the necessary courage to work through the fearful parts our grief.

I think I am beginning to understand why grief feels like suspense. It comes from the frustration of so many impulses that had become habitual. So many roads once; now so many culs de sac.

—C.S. Lewis,
A Grief Observed

FAITHFUL COURAGE

The path to courage is blazed by fear,
We can't have one unless the other's near.
With faithfulness, then, toward each we'll steer,
Embracing both and holding them dear.

4

When I was seven years old, I wrote my first poem. It was about my pet snapping turtle. I found him lumbering across a street in my neighborhood. I kept him for just a few days, long enough though, to name him Yurtle, consider him my pet, and discover his fondness for bologna. My sisters and I loved watching him take bites out of a fresh slice of the tidy pink meat. His mouth was like a bird's beak and his neck would stretch out slowly from beneath his heavy shell and in a quick snap, a perfect triangular piece would be gone from our special offering. After several bites, the bologna looked almost like a star. Yurtle was fun and entertaining. And we had a seemingly endless supply of bologna that could keep this relationship going for a long time.

One day, my older sister and I decided that Yurtle should be set free, to roam again the excitement of our neighborhood lawns and puddles. The very next morning as we crossed the street to go to school, we saw Yurtle. He hadn't stayed in the safety of the yards, as we'd envisioned. Instead, it appeared, he'd headed right for the street and didn't survive the crossing. I felt immediately shocked and saddened at what had happened, then guilty for my part in the apparent bad decision to simply set him free. What had happened to Yurtle was gruesome and it seemed so unfair. Shortly after that I discovered the therapeutic value of poetry. In school we were assigned to write a poem. I titled mine "Yurtle the Turtle." The last lines are all I remember now, but I do recall feeling some comfort in writing and reading it:

Yurtle the turtle lived in a window well,
Yurtle the turtle was swell.

It was a poem about grieving and accepting a loss. I didn't know it at the time, but my own feelings had no place to go. A dead turtle—especially a squashed, road kill one—just wasn't something anyone cared to hear about. No big deal, right? But Yurtle had been my pet, my responsibility for a short time, and I'd blown it. The poem helped me move through this relatively minor grief and validate the loss, regardless of its magnitude in the bigger world. Just seeing the word, "was," helped me accept the reality of what happened and that regardless of Yurtle's importance to anyone else in the universe, he'd mattered to me. Sometimes, you must grieve alone.

There's one other thing worthy of note about Yurtle. The fact that I'd taken the time to grieve and reflect gave me another perspective. I realized another possibility was that I'd actually saved his life for a while. After all, I did find him in the street to start with. Who's to say I didn't prevent him from getting run over by a car the day I brought him home? And he got to have a nice feast of bologna for several days before he met his destiny. Thanks to my opportunity to create a poem, I was able to acknowledge my regrets, realize the loss, grieve it, gain a new perspective, and just plain feel better. A good poem can help you see and feel something that ordinary words cannot.

One might think that given all the therapeutic value discovered in writing poetry about a lost turtle, I would have continued such writing. The poem had been a school assignment to complete, so even though I discovered benefits from doing it, I stopped. No new poems were assigned, so none were created.

It never occurred to me to write a poem again until I worked for a small educational software company twenty-five years later. Product development was more costly than expected and I could see the need for a group morale boost was high. As national sales manager, I decided that just because we were short on money didn't mean we would be short on creativity. This gave birth to my first poem since Yurtle. I began the company's first national sales meeting with a humorous poetic "roast" that captured all the software bugs, missed deadlines, financial fears, challenges, and frustrations of the group. These rhyming boosters became part of all our national meetings because of the power they contained to elevate morale, energy and the ability to cope with continued challenges.

It wasn't until I became fully engaged in my therapy training that I experienced the more serious and profound healing power of poetry. Not only were we dissecting our own life stories and histories, but those of our colleagues and clients as well. I was profoundly shaken by the countless stories of abuse and neglect. My poetry writing grew to help me cope. One person's story in particular began the serious therapeutic poetry I do today; I will call her Pat.

Pat was grieving the recent death of her father. He had abused Pat in countless ways throughout her childhood, which included frequently calling her "garbage." Pat's grief was more excruciatingly painful because of his use of these same words to her on his deathbed. Now she battled suicidal thoughts and overusing alcohol to numb her pain. She talked about her life seeming like a flame in a lantern. When she felt most suicidal, the flame image grew dim, nearly extinguishing altogether. My poem for Pat in this book is called "Rejecting the Darkness." I share this brief summary about Pat because she was grieving many losses and overcoming such tremendous challenges, yet she continued to pursue and find hope.

Jessica June. Jessie was the beautiful, sweet young woman we had come to believe might be our son's wife some day. She died suddenly and unexpectedly of a pulmonary embolism at age twenty-four. I cannot even begin to adequately write about Jessie, her hopes and dreams, struggles and successes, her precious giggle and sweet disposition. But the poems of grief and loss insistently poured out. Publishing was repeatedly suggested, but I was afraid.

Poetry can be so many things: beautiful, lively, healing, hopeful, encouraging, funny. But it's frightening, too, very personal, and not mainstream. It is in remembrance of Jessie's spirit that I share these poems. "Jessie's Message" came as an answer to a prayer, when I'd asked God for help seeing what had happened to her in the sudden, unexpected moments of her death.

Jessie was an answer-seeker, with an independent heart, and she fought her fears. It is in the spirit of fear fighting that Jessie and I once talked about, that I fight my own fears about publishing my poetry. She wanted to make a positive contribution in life and it is my prayer that these poems are our way of partnering together to help make a positive difference for others.

"Blessed are those who mourn,
for they will be comforted."
             (Matthew 5:4)

Your eyes may not have seen the trip God created just for me;
Before you saw that I had gone, Jesus held me on His knee.

My tears had formed to say goodbye, but before even one could fall,
I gazed into my Savior's eyes and heard His gentle call.

His loving arms embraced me as He took away my tears;
He said He'll always love me and that you should have no fears.

He's prepared a place for us to meet that's glorious and pure;
I'm happy now and will be then, of that you can be sure.

Given that grieving can be such a confusing and painful time full of many unknowns, it can be like crossing a bridge in a fog. We aren't sure what is on the other side. An awareness of grief's stages can be helpful. It is equally important, however, to keep them in perspective. They do not progress in a hard and fast sequence, nor move in a single, linear direction.

Elizabeth Kubler-Ross identified five stages that dying and grieving people experience:

Shock/Denial; Anger; Depression; Bargaining; Acceptance

These stages came to also be used in discussions of grieving any loss. It is best to view them, not as an assignment to achieve, but as a process that flows back and forth. Information about grief's motion can help us see that there is some progression to the grieving process and that the intensity of its early suffering is not permanent.

Terence P. Curley, in *The Ministry of Consolers*, identifies three phases of grief:

1. **Separation**—Disorienting numbness, shock, avoidance, or denial
2. **Transition**—Multiple emotions, disorganization, transition
3. **Reorganization**—Readjusting to and accepting the loss

It is comforting to know you are not going crazy. That is one of the advantages of learning about grief stages. In *Transforming Loss*, John Schneider, PhD, reminds us, "We don't 'get over' a significant loss, but we can move on. Instead of getting over what we lost, we incorporate its meaning and its memory into the fabric of the rest of our lives."

C.S. Lewis, in *A Grief Observed* said, "For in grief nothing 'stays put.' One keeps on emerging from a phase, but it always recurs. Round and round. Everything repeats. Am I going in circles or dare I hope I am on a spiral?"

The reality is that the phases of grief flow back and forth and tend not to be helped when anyone tries to hurry them along, stay stuck in them, or deny them entirely. It is common to feel numbness and disbelief in early stages, but that can return even in later periods, possibly triggered by an anniversary or other life stressors. Finding ways to stay connected to our loved ones and our own needs is important at all stages of grief.

In the poem "Good Grief," we see what can happen if we try to over-analyze our grief or try to force it to follow a prescribed pattern.

Books say grief comes in stages; well sometimes I think it's true.
The first one is denial, but right now I am so blue.
Oh, that comes after anger, good grief—I can't get it right!
So after I am mad, then sad, is acceptance in sight?

Only after I've done bargaining, the book is telling me,
That I can accept this painful loss, good grief, must I agree?
No, I must not, but yet I may, for one thing I feel sure;
No matter what stage I am in, I know I must endure.

Forget it! I don't want to, so right back to denial I go.
I can't believe my loved one's gone; I'm just sure it can't be so.
Then I wake up to another day, my thoughts have changed again;
I feel some peace, I don't know why, in simple remembering when...

They may come out of order, and predictable they're not;
Grief "stages" may move back and forth, with none that should be fought.
For as we suffer through our loss, in grief we can also find,
All new dimensions of our love and connections that are kind.

In the early weeks following the loss of a loved one, painful emotions seem to dominate our being. We are forced to deal with the shocking reality of our loved one's absence in our life and the many dimensions associated with the loss. At times, even a sense of hopelessness or despair can seem to be our new forever reality. But it is important to know the intensity of such sadness is not permanent. In our fast-paced, achievement-oriented society, we may feel we are failing or even going crazy. These are common feelings, so try not to judge yourself harshly or apply societal timetables to your personal experience of grief.

OCEAN OF EMOTION

We rarely know the depths of our soul,
Until loss plays its hazardous role.
Emotions plunge as deep as the sea,
And into the sky we want to flee.
Then comes a day we know we'll make it through;
Crashing waves have calmed, transforming the view.

Emotions, especially new and unfamiliar ones, can be frightening in their intensity. "Ocean of Emotion" captures the depth and ferocious aspect of grief. The sheer variety, intensity and unpredictability of such emotions can truly make you want to flee them. But neither "flight nor fight" makes them vanish and can instead cause new waves of emotion to come crashing into our experience of loss, prolonging the difficulty. If we learn to accept the flow and motion of our emotion, the waves do calm and our view eventually transforms into a more serene and less painful one.

Some journeys you have to make alone;
The pathway of grief you make your own.

It may be eased when a love's light is shown
To help you go on instead of postpone.

One truth exists, off-course you'll be thrown;
Your dreams have changed, though to what is unknown.

Grief's route and timing some may not condone;
You may even sense a disapproving tone.

That can't be your guide through this difficult zone;
Inner faith and courage is how you are grown.

Some describe grieving as being caught in a forceful storm that blows us about so fiercely that we cannot emerge from it unchanged. Every grief experience is unique, even if we have a shared loss with someone close to us. We may have some common experiences with others in grief, which is comforting, but it doesn't eliminate our suffering or our need to navigate through. Usually there is some altered way of viewing and living life after a significant loss. Our society appears unsympathetic in many ways, so it is up to us to make our way through these changes. Faith and courage become our vital allies.

When a child or young person dies, grief also bears an overwhelming sense of betrayal. The natural order of things has been thrown off and the feeling of injustice complicates grief. As expressed in the poem "Grieving Hearts," we may feel numb from the shock.

Sometimes guilty feelings invade our minds over things we didn't get done, or the conversations that never happened because we believed there would be more time to do so in the future. Grieving, no matter the loss, involves forgiving ourselves for what didn't get done, even if it would not have been possible to anticipate the loss or do everything we wished we could have done had the future not been taken away from the relationship. Poetry offers one of many creative outlets that can soothe us during our grief.

GRIEVING HEARTS

I do not know how it can be;
This child is gone instead of me.
So much ahead, so much to come,
That future gone makes our hearts numb.

I knew her heart, but not enough;
You'll have more time, was my mind's bluff.
She never leaves this aching heart;
Who could have known we'd have to part?

These poems come to help us cope;
We'll hold her soul and cling to hope.
For there is beauty in this, to;
Lives touching lives as angels flew.

When the expected natural order of things is upset by a premature death, it can be particularly devastating to older people, who often feel they should have died first.

"A Young Leader" shares the shock and struggle of such an experience, along with a healthy resolution that we can learn from, and be led by, these young souls in a spiritually uplifting way.

A Young Leader

None of us ever thought it would be you
Leading the way to the next life's view.
It seemed your life had just begun,
And was so far from being done.

We are the elders, so unprepared,
For youth gone first, a thought never dared.
We assumed we'd be the ones to lead,
An order in life and death to heed.

But these are things beyond our control;
You've led the way, so we'll follow your soul.
Your life is now enfolded in ours,
And over us your spirit towers.

CHILDREN

We lived, in part, just to see their smiles,
To lose ourselves in their needs and styles.
Their faces fill our hearts and special frames,
And they never let us forget to play some games.

Some joys they brought whizzed right on by;
Busy days vanished, tucked in with a sigh.
If they leave this earth before we do...
We'll leave it to God to help us through.

We may always feel some disbelief
That we are left with so much grief.
They would not want us to stop all play,
So with their spirit, we'll find a way!

"We don't stop playing because
we grow old ...
we grow old because
we stop playing."
—George Bernard Shaw

It is impossible to fully express the agony of losing a child. It has been said that when parents die, we are grieving a large part of the past, and when a child dies; we grieve for the past, but even more for the lost future. "Parents' Hearts" reflects the inconsolable suffering of losing a child. An encouragement to continuing the connection with caring people and the spirit of the lost child brings a ray of hope for the future.

We hold each other in our disbelief;
A kiss, a hug, might it bring some relief?

Yes, some, but not where the deepest hurt lies,
That truth is spoken in both of our eyes.

But in our reaching and touching, we feel
An angel's presence that will help us heal.

25

Receiving validation in our grief is one of our most important needs. Whether that comes in prayer, therapy, or from a friend, it can help us mend. Healing is something difficult to identify and nearly impossible to measure, but the combination of helpful people, places, ceremonies, and things often becomes the foundation of new hope.

Every loss that becomes part of our life's journey carves out a new life for us. It may create significant change or just modify a small element of our everyday life, but many people find that thinking of it as a new life can help them continue on. Endings always bring beginnings, even if they weren't part of our wishes or our plans.

"Good Mourning Friends," shows us the pleasant surprise that can be part of discovering the caring people we encounter or a reconnection with our spiritual life that helps us as we mourn.

GOOD MOURNING FRIENDS

So many things are happening when our hearts are in grief,
At times we feel despair that goes beyond our belief.

"How can we take this suffering?" is our question that cries out,
And sometimes when it is at its peak, a friend shows us the route.

A quiet chat, a heartfelt note, or a story that is shared,
becomes the path that shows the way, just knowing someone cared.

For our loss has brought new hearts to us to help our spirits rise;
The love that's shared between us is a mighty pleasant surprise.

27

Thank you for listening to me, friend;
Your quiet acceptance has helped me mend.
Sometimes you cry, too, simply moving your head;
You give up the words and give love pats instead.

You don't tell me to hurry, get busy, or rush,
And you've never told me to be quiet or hush.
Our tears open us up for laughter as well,
How that's helped us both heal is hard to tell.

But healing is not something we have to measure;
We're grateful for friendship that we'll always treasure.

28

Often we are both griever and consoler, as loved ones mourning the same loss. One of the greatest gifts we can give and receive is to simply listen and be listened to. There are rarely perfect words to say, but there are words that can make grief more difficult. This is not the time for giving advice, criticism, distasteful jokes, or pep talks. These things can be taken the wrong way and be hurtful. Quiet listening is often the most helpful.

Their presence, once, was a fragrant embrace that let us touch delight.
Their absence, now, is the unwelcome guest we wish not to invite.

Get along now, void, can't you go away? It's time that you take flight!
Can't you replace this aching emptiness with something full, yet light?

Surely that would make this heaviness leave and bring back what feels right;
Time ushers in some fleeting moments now, faith puts the rest in sight.

"Mourning Flight" acknowledges the feelings of emptiness and heaviness that accompany grief, and expresses the desire to flee them both. We often have contradictory wishes when grieving, seen in the poem's request to fill the emptiness full, yet keeping it light.

We may experience a mournful sense that nothing feels right. But we are also left with new hope, as we feel fleeting moments of peacefulness, with the possibility of more to come, in "faith puts the rest in sight." It is helpful to try and notice those moments of feeling better, fleeting as they may be in the early stages, as a builder of future hope.

I had to say your name;
At first a whisper,
Then another, not so quiet.

I had to call your name;
A whisper was not enough.
With flooding tears, my cry came louder.

I had to wail your name;
Loudly, mournfully
Alone, breathless, yet breathing.

I had to wail your name;
Rejecting my contained grief
Releasing a sorrow not meant to be tame.

I had to wail your name;
To connect with you,
With my soul, with God, with life.

I had to wail your name;
To breathe deeply
And to heal.

Perhaps because we believe it is expected of us, we try to contain our sorrow and our natural reactions to it. We may feel it is crazy or inappropriate to let out our grief, even if we're completely alone. We experience physical symptoms such as tightness in our chest, body aches, difficulty breathing, yet we persist in trying to hold our grief in.

Some people fear that if they start to cry, they won't be able to stop. But that's just not true. Crying spells have a natural cessation. Trust your body and soul on this. "Wail Your Name" reveals one of many possible releases. You, too, may feel a need to cry out your loved one's name while allowing your natural tears to flow. Go ahead and cry; go ahead and wail. You'll relieve your body's physical tensions of grief. We need to remember to give ourselves permission to quit being so tame. We need to remember we are not crazy; we are grieving.

Burning tears, like a scalding lava flow,
With each release there is some letting go.

But they do not harden like the jagged black rock,
Instead, they soften, allowing hearts to unlock.

Our tears warm a path to help us navigate through;
Slow motion is flowing to form what is new.

"God wants our tears," a dear friend once told me when I was grieving and couldn't stop the tears, and had apologized for them. She wouldn't let me apologize, which was a wonderful gift for me in that moment. I'd judged that I should be done with the crying. It was years later that I read about the healing chemicals in tears of grief. Tears are good medicine. They are evidence of strength, not weakness. People also often experience serenity and physical relief when they allow their tears to flow. In "Healing Tears," I share the many benefits of tears. Trust their healing power.

"Holding On" speaks the raw truth of how unbearable the shock of losing a loved one can feel, especially if it was sudden or unexpected. There are physical, as well as mental ailments in grief. Sleeplessness, aches, fatigue, and even vomiting are not uncommon. Many people question whether they indeed can bear to live with their loss. Some imagine escape routes from their loss or a wish they could simply join their lost loved one.

Parents who have lost a child may wish they could trade places with their child to make the natural order fit how it "should be." It takes effort to continue on, but as we see in the poem, there is hope in simple comforts that can come from inspiring words, quiet closeness with someone we trust, music, or in connecting with nature's beauty.

HOLDING ON

I cannot stand to bear this loss,
Stop telling me that it's the boss!
Just make things like they used to be;
Please bring my loved one back to me.

The hole's too big, I cannot breathe;
It must mean that I, too, should leave.
I'll go to them, I'll find a way,
I start to plan the time, the day.

Just when that's all I can conclude,
A sunset calms my anguished feud.
A loving voice shares words of strength;
There's new life here, at any length.

It's maddening that loss makes us grow,
And helps us see where we can go.

Ceremonies can help us see and feel the differences in letting go and holding on. These phrases have taken on so many meanings in our everyday language that trying to grasp them in our grief process can become very confusing. The poem, "Letting Go," reveals the healthy movement from a lack of acceptance to the realization that holding on drains our energy.

Although holding on is a natural part of the grief experience, it will eventually give way to letting go. Letting go does not mean ceasing to care or abandoning memories of our loved one. It means we become less resistant to the change our loss has brought about. It helps us conserve our energy as we incorporate the loss into the fabric of our lives.

LETTING GO

Dear loved one, I am letting you go now;
Holding on had been my secretive vow.

Tight and insistent, we'd refused to part.
Conspiring like this, I'd not have to start

To accept your absence as life goes on;
This deal could continue from dusk 'til dawn.

Now I know letting go still keeps you near,
For your heart lives in many, always here.

The dimensions of loss must be taken in layers,
For if they came all at once, we'd lose faith in our prayers.

The absence of our loved one hits us with countless surprises;
The many things we miss seem to come in all shapes and sizes.

The way they liked to hold a spoon, or fold a towel just so,
Were things we barely ever noticed before they had to go.

They gave us big companionship we miss in a big way;
We dream about them coming back and wishing they could stay.

Their special tailored voices when talking to our pet,
Gave us little pleasures we now try not to forget.

As time goes by the layers change and we find joy in new ways;
We are grateful for our memories and all our special days.

In "Dimensions of Loss," we see an example of the many layers of daily experiences, self-identities, feelings, and future plans that we miss when we experience a significant loss or dramatic change in our life. Reminders of varying new aspects of the loss can come several times daily in the early stages, often catching us by surprise. Thankfully, these realizations of loss do not come all at once, for such a flood of awareness could be too overwhelming.

It is helpful to remember that grief feelings don't always pop up at logical or convenient times. Awareness of additional dimensions of our loss is sometimes triggered by unrelated events that suddenly bring a flood of emotion that startles us. They are legitimate emotions that need no apology and it is okay to cry, even if it is years later.

In this poem, letting go is compared to forgiveness because of the similarities between the two. Both take tremendous courage and effort, but in the process, new possibilities emerge and rekindle hope.

There can be so many layers of disappointments with losing a loved one; it is rare to get through grief without uncovering some need for forgiveness. We may feel wronged or have found mistakes that leave a need to forgive doctors, relatives, funeral directors, or others, including ourselves, or even our departed loved one.

42

FORGIVENESS AND LETTING GO

Letting go of a lost loved one
Is like forgiveness in a way.

It doesn't mean that we'll forget,
Or that what happened is okay.

It does mean that we'll always try
To live a life that is fulfilled.

We'll not let bitter asking "Why?"
Make all our dreams vanish, stand–stilled.

We may even find brand new dreams
Start taking shape when we let go.

A higher spirit leads, it seems,
When we allow ourselves to grow.

Fond memories help us keep going;
Their power to comfort goes far.

Healed energy now is flowing,
When forgiveness beams like a star.

No two people grieve in the same way. Even parents grieving the devastating loss of a child will experience different dimensions of their grief. Everyone's verbal or other external displays and outlook for the future vary considerably.

With couples, these differences can complicate bereavement and cause feelings of isolation and conflict, making the loss even more painful to endure. It is important to recognize that having different responses to grief does not mean that one person is grieving incorrectly.

Couples need to find acceptable ways to communicate openly about some of their feelings, without expectations of an identical experience on the part of their partner. Not all feelings must be shared.

Similar mistaken expectations of family members or friends can cause feelings of isolation for grieving people when they do not receive a hoped-for response. This can happen with the loss of a pet, or even in a positive change such as a job promotion.

One of the challenges of grief is the paradox of needing to rely on people for some components of our grief, yet being self-reliant for others. The poems "Unique Journeys" and "Voice is a Choice" speak to these matters. Other people can be remarkably helpful, but we must also learn to find ways to validate and nurture our needs from within ourselves.

My body aches to share my grief with you;
For now, though, that's impossible to do.
I understand why you cannot join me
In that mournful place neither wants to be.

Our sense of this loss does not overlap;
We both move, alone, without any map.
Yet down the road we discover a space
For sharing, once again, a common place.

46

You were the one I thought would understand,
When I reached out for a comforting hand.
But the distance was too great, our worlds too far apart;
The phone just couldn't give us the needed place to start.

Some grief feelings aren't meant to find their way to our voice;
Silent reflection, at times, is our better personal choice.
Frightened by our solitude, the gift received becomes clear;
We've learned again that we can climb new mountains of our fear.

47

The poem, "Voice is a Choice," expresses the deep frustration and disappointment about the realization that some people will let us down during our grief journey. Rarely is a trusted friend or close family member trying to be unsupportive or cause further pain. But given the unique experience people have in their bereavement, these communication challenges and disappointments will occur in the normal encounters of the process.

It is a paradox, but sometimes the solo components of our grief journey can strengthen us and get us in touch with our own courage and ability to find comfort within ourselves. It can be healthy to think of these inevitable disappointments as a gift received that helps us "climb new mountains of our fear."

Especially in the early stages of loss, we may feel despair and a heightened need to have our closest friends or family members fully understand, even join us in our feelings. Sometimes that is possible, but often it is not. No matter how close you are to someone who is grieving the same loss, your feelings will not be identical.

Your relationship with your loved one was unique. You miss different aspects of what you once had, and these are not the same as any other person who is also grieving. In this regard, "Unique Journeys" conveys the lack of alignment that may exist in the early stages of loss, yet shines a ray of hope on the common place that might still be found down the road.

Great comfort can come from creating or keeping objects that symbolize the positive memories we want to preserve of our loved one. A woman in a grief group talked about the comfort she received from the quilt she made out of fabric from her son's shirts. Planting a garden, making a collage or small photo album from favorite photos and keepsakes can be therapeutic. Or simply keeping special objects in places where you can remember your loved one can be helpful. Our meanings and reactions to symbols often change over time.

Your cuff link sits on my windowsill;
It's almost like a happiness pill.
Except there's nothing I have to swallow;
To get relief from feeling hollow.

And all it takes is a little glance
To remind me how you used to dance.
It finds happy memories that are best,
And puts any others right to rest.

The varied meanings give me a smile,
When it links me to your special style.
One little look and I can rejoice
The time we had and our healing choice.

We held hands in your final hours;
The cuff link has grown healing powers.
Although at first it made me sad,
Just having it now makes me glad.

This poem is an example of how a tiny object can become a big healer when positive meaning is applied to it. Notice how it is not a reflection of the painful aspects of the loss, but rather that it preserves the joyful part of the relationship and the time that was shared.

Accepting the loss of a beloved person or thing isn't something that happens with ease. Rarely is it completed in one clear or singular identified moment. Acceptance is more like a patchwork of moments that somehow eventually piece themselves together to form a quilt of adequate comfort.

One of the things we can do to help ourselves continue to create these pieces of the quilt is to find our own ways to converse with, say farewell to, and honor our departed loved ones. Prayers, lighting a special candle in remembrance, tending a garden or plant, or creating a ceremony can all be powerful tools of healing.

I brought some flowers to the beach;
To say good-bye, for the sea I reach.
The petals dancing in a wave
Are a happier vision than your grave.

We even chuckled you and I,
For on wet rocks I'm not so spry.
I slipped and stumbled and thought I'd fall,
But nothing could stop this special call.

One petal left kept dancing back,
Making sure I'm not out of whack!
Your spirit lingered there a bit,
And told me I am not to quit.

That petal, too, then washed away,
And swept peace through another day.

The poem "Dancing Petals" shares part of an ocean ceremony. In a private ritual we can create a more pleasant visual memory than those that may have existed at the funeral or other formal functions. Rituals can leave us with a powerful impression that our loved ones have moved on in their afterlife. Making the decision to have your own private ceremony can in itself be healing. Your relationship with your loved one was unique. It stands to reason that your own personalized observance would offer comfort that only you can uniquely feel.

There is surprising value in speaking words out loud to communicate your sense of loss to nature, your loved one, or your God. The words do not have to be perfectly planned or articulated. You may feel a strong spiritual presence that you'd not expected. Words, images, or feelings may come to you that create a peacefulness you could not have anticipated. Some people sense they've received messages that give them courage and guidance for their future. These can all be profoundly comforting. "That petal, too, then washed away, and swept peace through another day."

53

FIRSTS

There are many firsts that will occur after the loss of our loved one. These can be special dates such as birthdays and anniversaries; they can be events, holidays, or seasonal changes, as in the poem, "First Snow." Acknowledgement of the date or event, whether expressed silently or to a friend, may be helpful. Depending on the significance of the event, a shared ceremony or ritual can be more comforting.

FIRST SNOW

The snow has fallen while we sleep;
When we awake, we sigh and weep.
Our numb limbs feel heavy, like the new fallen snow;
Weighed down by our grief, our energy is low.

For the first snow is beauty she always did love,
To share it with her now, we pray to heaven above.
As we gaze at the branches covered in white,
Her spirit touches us to say she's all right.

A lightness sweeps in and takes our heaviness away;
We arise to move about, seeing beauty in gray.

Autumn Angel

The colors are so vibrant on this lovely autumn day;
What is our angel doing now? I wonder and I pray.

Does she see the same bright colors with their many varied hues?
Or from heaven are they better, blessed with angels' special views?

I imagine that I see her flying slowly by the leaves,
Brushing in more radiant color while in and out she weaves.

I don't suppose I'll ever know until my day comes, too;
Until then, dear Lord I pray, keep our angel close to you.

They tell me I am dying;
That simply cannot be.

These doctors must be lying;
My family still needs me!

A treatment plan is forming;
Some comfort it will bring.

Inside I still am storming;
To hope, I plan to cling.

I watch my family's brave side;
Forgiveness happens, too.

This father now feels deep pride,
To know they'll make it through.

Hope transfers to my next life;
My spirit gets a lift.

Joy comes in place of my strife;
Heaven gives me a gift.

56

"A Father's Perspective" shares the dying person's experience of grief's stages: denial, anger, sadness, bargaining and acceptance. When death is due to a prolonged illness, there can be healing communication during that time, which becomes a gift not only to the dying person, but to the loved ones who grieve after the death.

If this type of communication was not possible, it can be helpful to write about what you would have said, and perhaps what you would have liked to hear, given the opportunity. Sometimes we have to grieve the lost opportunities for those conversations or the lost dreams for the future of the relationship.

We never know how good we are
until we are called to rise.
> —Emily Dickinson

When a pregnancy is lost, parents and family members grieve the loss of life and all the dreams that came with the expected birth and growth of a child. "A Tiny Soul" honors those fragile losses and embraces the memory of the cherished soul that will live on.

Dear unborn baby, I grieve for you so;
I yearn to hold you and to not let go.

Your tiny soul created many dreams;
Each one shining bright, like tiny sunbeams.

There were many more than I even knew;
Now they dance before me, crystal clear in view.

The loss of your life and these dreams we grieve,
Are as big as the world, yet hard to believe.

So as we mourn, we'll remember one thing;
Your tiny soul will live on, and joy, too, it will bring.

M ost of the *Rays of Hope* poems have been about grieving the loss of someone who has died. With other significant losses, the mourning experience shares similarities. This includes losses such as health, relationship endings, career changes or job loss, and family stage changes.

Some of these topics are explored below and will be done so at greater lengths in future *Rays of Hope* books. It can be helpful to substitute our identified losses as "loved ones" in the grieving process. Changes in lifestyle, status, roles, relationships, or even in lost habits can create grief.

When a significant relationship ends, it can feel as devastating as a death. It can be one of life's most profoundly sad, anxious, and troubling transitions. This is especially true when we did not expect the ending, and thus, were wholly unprepared.

In the poem "Starting Over," shock is expressed as feeling stripped bare stemming from a sense of lost identity. To recover and move on, acknowledging mistakes and learning from them is an important growth tool. Finding the courage to rebuild our life and identity as a single person brings valuable lessons that are the gift of courageous honesty.

As with a death, we often experience shock, numbness, anger, and regrets or remorse when a relationship ends. Even if you initiated the breakup, there is usually a surprising element of emptiness and lost identity to work through.

In the transformational experience of rebuilding, we can find many positive discoveries. This is especially true when courageous honesty allows admission of errors that can be resolved to prevent similar difficulties in future relationships that are "down the road."

STARTING OVER

We were a couple; each one was a part.
Now we are singles, each with a new start.
We feel stripped bare, our identity unknown
We're surprised at this part of being alone.

To find ourselves we look ahead and behind.
We hope we'll discover we like what we find.
We see some mistakes sprinkled with pain and regret,
But the good we are learning we will not forget.

All lives have value even while they're adrift,
The lessons received are honesty's gift.

Joan Mueller in, *Is Forgiveness Possible?* addresses the topic of anger as a natural part of forgiveness, saying, "What one needs to do with leftover anger is to give it a positive direction. Forgiveness leaves one with an anger which is without malice." It is possible for anger to be healthy when it helps create necessary boundaries that can protect us from being the target of further abuse. It can also be a positive energizing force that assists us in finding constructive solutions in our transitioning lives.

If anger creates extreme hostility and dangerous aggression, vengeful fantasies or behaviors, therapeutic intervention is needed so anger can be managed to prevent destruction of health and future relationships.

In broken relationships, the grief stages (denial, anger, depression, bargaining, acceptance) can apply similarly and be useful to remember, in some respects even more so than in death. Because a breakup involves choices that were made, sometimes one or both parties fail to reach the acceptance part of grieving the loss. Being aware of grief's stages can help us work through grief over a lost relationship.

In all things of nature there
is something of the marvelous.
—Aristotle

Some life transitions are due to happy events or successes, but they trigger emotions of grief because they involve the loss of many things we loved or enjoyed. This can occur with job promotions, getting married, having a baby or having children leave home to start their young adult lives. This can be complicated by a belief that we have no right to be sad, because it is a positive event or a goal achieved. Nonetheless, losses are involved, and although they are not due to tragedy, they are worth acknowledging.

When our primary role as parent has shifted due to children leaving home, the empty nest can trigger grief emotions. As with other losses, talking or writing about it may ease the way. In the poem "Growing Always," we see the tug of this transition. Punctuating the grief process with rituals and celebrations can help with this, too.

GROWING ALWAYS

It has come time again to change my mind;
Empty nest anew, can't be sure what I'll find.

I've seen my baby birds leave the nest to fly;
If I helped them soar, tell me why do I cry?

Perhaps it's never easy when a child must leave,
As parents we must find ways to celebrate and grieve.

Not all tears, we've learned, are about being sad,
Some are shed for nature's beauty and being glad;

That like the redwoods, children reach a new height,
Growing always toward heaven while finding their light.

Some jobs are lost by choice, as in a planned retirement, while others vanish abruptly due to layoffs caused by economic or political changes. Whether by choice or not, our work creates roles and identities for us that give us a sense of purpose. When the job ends, even when by choice and seen as a positive accomplishment of a goal, there can be a confusing adjustment period.

We may feel sorrow, anger, or emptiness, or sense we lack purpose as a result of the lost job. Similar to losing a relationship, we find we have to discover who we are in the context of the multiple changed roles and daily routines.

RETIRED AND REHIRED

I never thought I'd hear myself say,
"I miss my job almost every day."

I thought I'd love the loss of stress,
Of keeping time and chasing success.

Though true for a while, it wasn't to last,
I'd forgotten to change the "me" of the past.

So I began to rebuild my new I.D.
With talent and passion, I'd hire me!

To be the best of what I always was,
This transition, too, makes sense because

I can contribute based on love and skill,
Regardless of pay I have value still.

It's quite an adventure, adjusting to change,
But new meanings are found when we rearrange.

It is a tragic reality that many people have had to endure unspeakable abuses as children. A frequent result of abuse and abandonment is an inability to discern painful emotions. This becomes especially challenging in times of additional loss.

One of the problems with denying painful emotions, however, is it also numbs us from experiencing joy. We can see the struggle unfold in "Uncovering" and in "Rejecting the Darkness" as years of mistaken impressions about emotions tumble out.

UNCOVERING

Don't tell me to feel feelings, that simply wouldn't do.
I was taught to rise above them, ignoring that I'm blue.
Get off this kick, now will you? I'm fine, so leave me be!
Maybe some need feelings, but it surely isn't me.

I've got my life together, I am emotion—free.
I deny unwanted feelings; strong people know that's the key.
Don't tell me I am grieving, I haven't time for that!
If I feel any pain now, I'll get stuck right where I'm at.

Good people see the bright side, doesn't that mean skip the tears?
Isn't it weak and selfish, to cry about loss or fears?
If I don't block these feelings, that might mean I must change,
But I'm not sure I'm ready for something so new and strange.

Did you say I'd feel joy, too, if I'd dare to let grief in?
Could that be what these tears are, rolling down over my grin?

REJECTING THE DARKNESS

Dearest Pat was always a beautiful child;
Sweet voice, heart a song, and disposition mild.
I can see her grace as she plays in the sun,
With a smile so radiant, she's the brightest one.

Some people noticed and valued her light,
But the one she needed most was as dark as night.
And try as she might to shine on his path,
All he could reflect was his own inner wrath.

Tender child, please know he had to light his own way
Not you, not the stars, nor the sun's brightest ray.
Precious one, you've always had so much to give,
Come out of the darkness and let yourself live.

Your light has not left you, it flickers about,
And though it feels dim now, it will not go out.
For the strength it had once is still a warm glow,
A gift from your self in a bright, shiny bow!

Stop running, keep healing, and soon you will feel,
Your light has grown brighter—it's safe to be real.
That warm glow you sought "serves you up" from within;
There's none, but your self, that you've had to win.

Though the scared child you were, found no comfort or rest,
You've now found good souls, who offer it with zest.
Stick with the people who've an inner glow, too,
For they can reflect back your light on to you!

A new beginning came from following my heart,
What a frightening place for a good girl to start!

I'd become so skilled at following orders;
I'd lost my true self, confined in others' borders.

But an insistent voice kept knocking down my walls,
It wouldn't allow me to continue my stalls.

It took every excuse and said, "That can't stop you!"
And it pumped in new courage that was long overdue.

It got me moving, taking steps I'd never dared,
And to my amazement, I kept going while scared.

Transitions bring challenges worth laboring through,
For they can give birth to an awesome new you!

John Fox, in his book *Poetic Medicine*, encourages reading and writing poems, saying, "Reading poems you enjoy may plant seeds for your own writing when the time is ripe."

I encourage you to read the poem, "Rhythm Falls," as an invitation to write, or continue writing, your own poems. Remember, poems don't have to rhyme or have a perfect rhythm. As the writer, let the words flow in whatever way feels most true, soothing, or comforting. Like the dancing water in the falls, dancing words can create a therapeutic surprise. In that spirit, any writing can provide insights you hadn't expected.

Rhythm Falls

When you get stuck it helps to rhyme,
And take a little trip through time.
Remembering love, a special touch,
Of someone you have missed so much.

Just grab your mood and write it down,
And let the rhyme make you a clown.
Or see if it can help you out
When you are sad or full of doubt.

Sometimes it even moves your soul,
And lifts you out of a dark hole.
Rhythm falls in a steady beat;
It's always fun to keep it neat.

It's okay, though, to mess it up,
And frolic words like a young pup.
As long as you find that surprise
Of dancing words before your eyes.

74

One of the most helpful and comprehensive books about grief I recommend is called *Finding My Way: Healing and Transformation Through Loss and Grief* by John Schneider, PhD. In it, he suggests three primary questions as a guide for discovery of our own grief awareness process:

What is lost?

What is left?

What is possible?

Although these questions are short and simple, moving through their many dimensions is neither. It takes courage and commitment to work through their many answers, but writing our responses to these and other questions in a journal can offer tremendous insight into our own losses.

Journal entries will change as we continue moving through our grief, as our perspectives continue to evolve. It can help us restore our sense of balance and organize the chaos that engulfs us while we mourn. In writing about what is possible, we can discover positive aspects of life again.

> *When we discover within ourselves the essence of our love*
> *after losing its external form, life has cause for celebration.*
> —*John M. Schneider, PhD*

You have probably heard of aromatherapy. Let's give "a-rhyme-a-therapy" a try! This is my word to describe the therapeutic benefits of writing poetry. Poems can provide sustenance and help us keep moving on through difficult times.

Every poem begins with one line. When we experience strong feelings and raw emotions, poetry gives us creative permission to cry out from the depth of our being.

If you feel uncertain about how to begin your poem (or journal entry), you can start with a sentence stem:

I miss _____

I remember when _____

How can it be that _____

Complete the thought and then keep adding what comes to you. You may discover great pleasure in the nourishing surprise of finding words that rhyme and fit perfectly a feeling that otherwise seemed to have no words (or took too many words to even attempt to convey).

Maintaining a certain rhythm can also provide structure that, at times, creates a perspective that heightens clarity. Sometimes, in obedience to a certain rhythmic pattern, we may happen upon bits of our unconscious wisdom. We may surprise ourselves by saying something we hadn't intended at all, yet it becomes a powerful ally in our own healing.

Of course, the nice thing about poetry is it doesn't have to rhyme or even keep a steady beat. It can free flow. It's all about personal preference; so do give it a try.

Let's use one of the sample sentence stems to provide an example of both:

> I miss the way we used to share a meal;
> Now, without you, I'm not sure I can heal.
> I remember how we'd share a quiet talk,
> And after our meal we'd go for a walk.

Or

> I miss sharing meals with you,
> Sitting quietly,
> Talking about our day;
> Sharing walks, sharing everything.

In the samples above, I've expressed similar thoughts in different forms. Writing helps uncover what is lost and can lead to discovering what is left and what is possible. This exercise can help you identify and accept many dimensions of your loss. Studies show that simply acknowledging in written form what our stress is lightens it to some extent.

> *Poetry provides guidance, revealing what you did not know you knew before you wrote or read the poem. This moment of surprising yourself with your own words of wisdom or of being surprised by the poems of others is at the heart of poetry as healer.*
>
> *—John Fox, Poetic Medicine*

Feel free to experiment in your journaling with all forms of writing. Explore how the different forms make you feel. You will discover the style that most helps you integrate the fragmented parts of your life and provide a place for both painful and joyful feelings to be held. This can light the way to your vision of where you've been, where you are, and where you are going. Your writing is for you.

Read and re-read your own or others' writing if you discover it helps you feel comforted or find courage to continue on your path in life. As with repeated viewing of a favorite movie, you will be amazed at the new things you notice with each additional reading of a poem that touched your heart.

Throughout our lives, we accumulate many losses. Grief is described as "a natural internal response to a significant loss that is experienced physically, emotionally, mentally and spiritually" by the Center for Grief and Loss in Saint Paul, Minnesota. It impacts our entire being and is a complex human experience.

If we are not able or allowed to grieve past losses, we take pieces of them into each new loss. It is very possible that whatever loss you are currently experiencing, you are actually grieving losses from long ago as well.

It may be time to acknowledge grief of the past. Ask yourself, "Are there other losses from the past I need to grieve right now?" Write out your answers. Keep this in mind in your "good mourning journey," and allow yourself to be creative as you move toward transformation. Like Pat, you can discover tools, people, and faith that help you light your way, even in times of darkness.

Your light has not left you, it flickers about.
And though it feels dim now, it will not go out.
For the strength it had once is still a warm glow,
A gift from your self in a bright, shiny bow!

It is my hope that this book has nourished your grieving heart and given you courage, comfort, and rays of hope in your own exploration through grief.

And now she's become the brightest twinkling star,
Shining down, so very close and yet so far.
So she pays us little visits as a butterfly, too,
Lighting close, bringing smiles, making us brand new.

Nobody has ever measured, even the poets,
how much a heart can hold.

—Zelda Fitzgerald

Albom, Mitch. *Tuesdays With Morrie: An Old Man, A Young Man, and Life's Greatest Lesson*. Doubleday, New York, NY, 1997

Cherry, Frank, and James, John W. *The Grief Recovery Handbook*. Harper & Row Publishers, Inc., New York, NY, 1988

Curley, Terence P. *The Ministry of Consolers*. The Liturgical Press, Collegeville, MN, 2004

Fisher, Bruce. *Rebuilding: When Your Relationship Ends*. Impact Publishers, San Luis Obispo, CA, 1981

Fox, John. *Poetic Medicine: The Healing Art of Poem-Making*. Penguin Putnam Inc, New York, NY, 1997

Kroen, William C. *Helping Children Cope with the Loss of a Loved One: A Guide for Grownups*. Free Spirit Publishing Inc., Minneapolis, MN 1996

Lewis, C. S. *A Grief Observed*. HarperCollins Publishers, New York, NY, 1961, 1996

Mueller, Joan. *Is Forgiveness Possible?* The Liturgical Press, Collegeville, MN, 1956

Schneider, John M. *Finding My Way: Healing and Transformation Through Loss and Grief*. Seasons Press, Colfax, WI, 1994

Schneider, John M. *Transforming Loss: A Discovery Process*. Integra Press, East Lansing, MI, 2004

Inever knew I would publish my poems. I want to thank Jessie's parents, Mike and Jackie, for their courage, love, and inspiration. What an honor to dedicate the book to your beautiful daughter.

To my son, Jamison, who has kindly confided aspects of his grief journey with me and suggested publishing "a poetry book."

To my daughter, Katie, for sharing our Redwoods trip and photographs for the book.

To my husband, Steve, my best friend who has so often been my "Ray of Hope."

To my family, friends, and colleagues who read the book manuscript and encouraged me to publish, and to the participants in my seminars for their feedback about the poems and therapeutic information in the book.

To my publishers, Sharron Stockhausen for her editing and listening skills, and to Harry Stockhausen for getting the technical parts of the book completed.

Susan Zimmerman, ChFC, LMFT is a Licensed Marriage and Family Therapist and Chartered Financial Consultant who has been helping people with life transitions and planning for over 20 years. She is an author and speaker on many topics related to finance and psychology. Susan has been featured in several publications, including the *Washington Post, LA Times, First for Women*, and the *St. Paul Pioneer Press*.

About DVT (from Coalition to Prevent Deep-Vein Thrombosis)

"Deep-vein thrombosis (DVT) and pulmonary embolism (PE) together comprise one of the nation's leading causes of death. DVT occurs when a blood clot forms in a deep vein, usually in the lower limbs. A complication of DVT, pulmonary embolism, can occur when a fragment of a blood clot breaks loose from the wall of the vein and migrates to the lungs, where it blocks a pulmonary artery or one of its branches."

For more information, please visit *www.preventdvt.org*.

Give the gift of courage, comfort and hope to help people through their transitions and grief.

Go to *www.ahaplan.com* for:
- Email contact
- Ordering information
- Quantity discounts
- Seminars or consultation
- Other books by Susan

ACT/ZFG
14530 Pennock Avenue
Apple Valley, MN 55124
Phone: 952-432-4666 (Twin Cities, MN);
or 800-525-5301 (US)
FAX: 952-432-6705

SHARE YOUR STORY

Please share your story about how *Rays of Hope in Times of Loss* has helped you. Write us at the above web or postal address. Thank you!

THOUGHTS
